A Mark Dahle Portfolio

Amanda Gets A Neighbor

(#4 in the series "Amanda Wanted A Miracle")

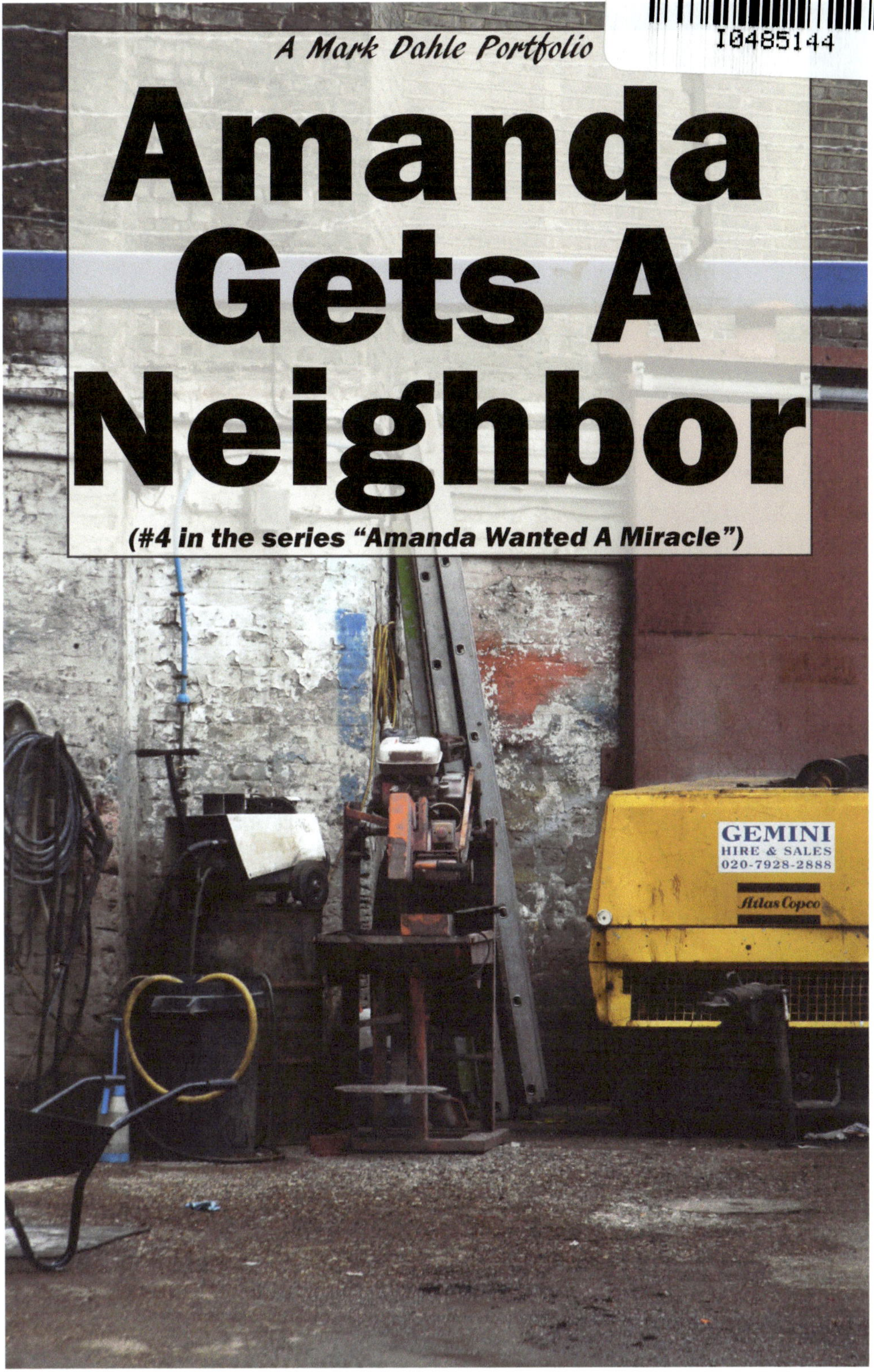

This is the fourth story in the series "Amanda Wanted A Miracle."
The books in this series:
1. Amanda Gets A Pumpkin
2. Amanda Gets A Watermelon
3. Amanda Gets A Surprise
4. Amanda Gets A Neighbor
5. Amanda Gets A Miracle

~ ~ ~

Mark Dahle Portfolios can be read in a few minutes and enjoyed for a lifetime.

Unlike many picture books, the text in this book is not related to the art. This might seem weird at first. One thing that makes it better is to order more portfolios until you get used to it. Fortunately, space is provided on the pages for you to draw your own pictures if you like.

This portfolio includes a beautiful 36 x 24 inch painting (at the right), twenty-five great photos from London, and a story about Amanda, who wanted a miracle but got a neighbor instead.

Photographs in this book are available in limited editions. See http://www.MarkDahle.com for more information and for previews of upcoming portfolios.

We do our best to create portfolios free of editing mistakes. If we miss anything, we reward people who report errors. For details see MarkDahle.com/Typos.html or email MarkDahle@aol.com with the subject line "Typos." Thanks!

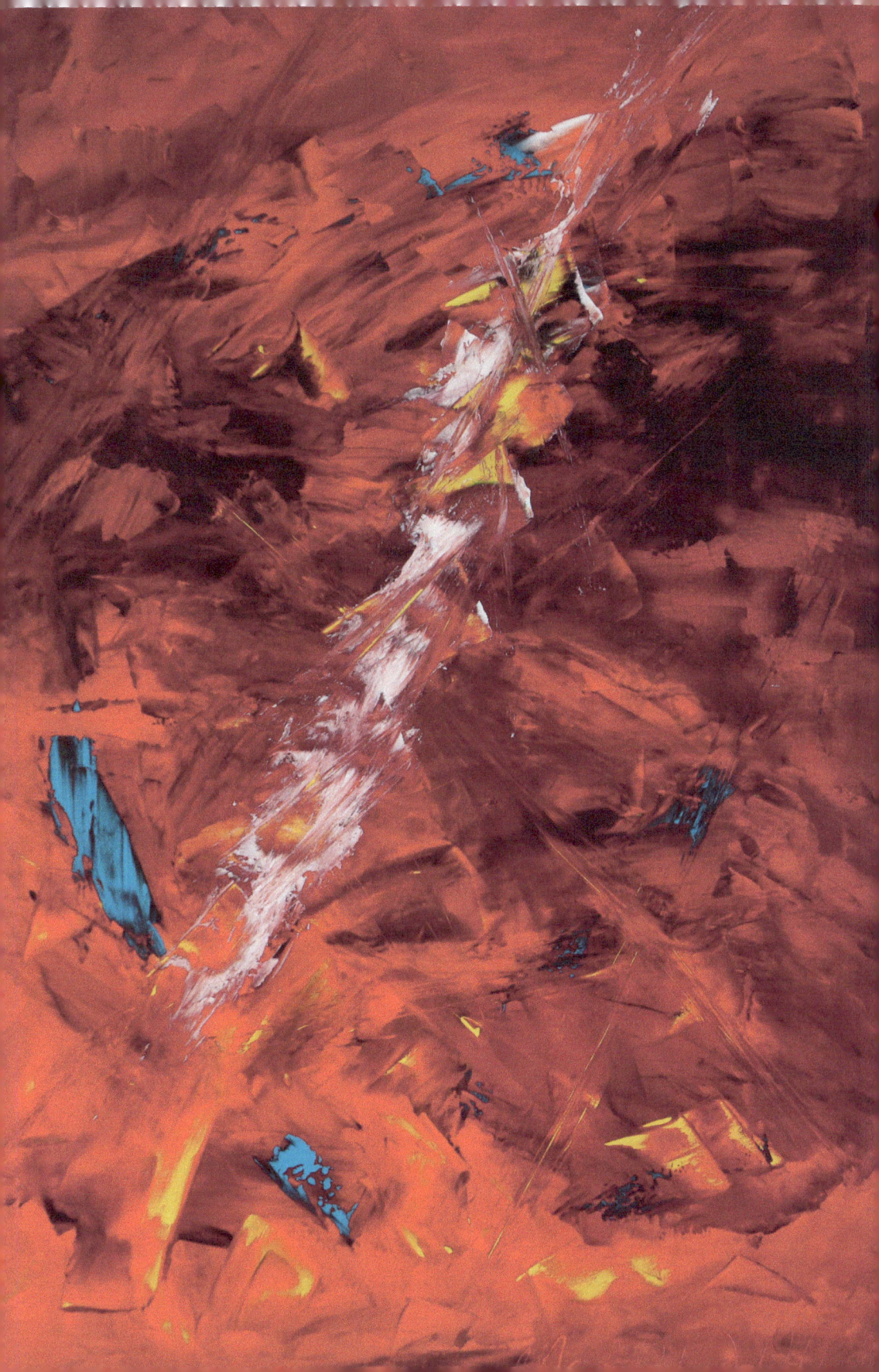

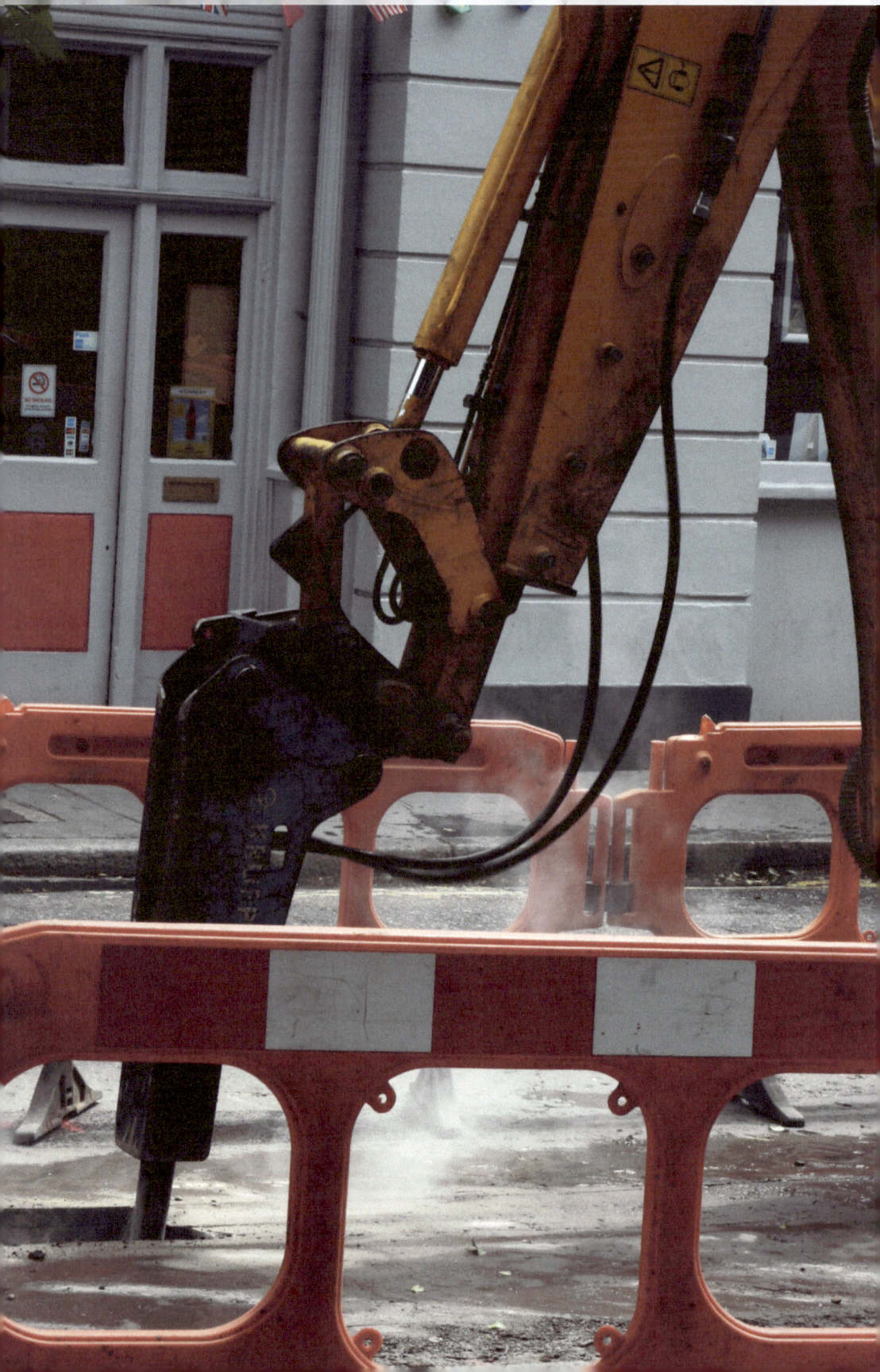

Amanda wanted a miracle. She had not had much success so far. But she was getting closer. At least she hoped so. She had two mysterious plants growing in her garden that showed some promise. She had one mysterious plant growing in her grandfather's garden. And she had learned from her grandfather that she had already touched the miracle she wanted. In fact, she had touched it many times – she just hadn't recognized it and had let it go. Now at least she knew what her miracle felt like, and the next time she bumped into it she was determined to hang on.

Waking up with sunlight streaming through her bedroom window, Amanda wiggled her toes and smiled and stretched and tossed the covers into a heap and sprang from the bed.

It was her third day back after the week at her grandfather's house, and she was anxious to see how much her plants had grown.

She dressed quickly and slipped on her shoes without tying the laces and raced out the door without shutting it. Then she reversed course, charged back, shut the door, and once more sprinted out to the garden, her laces flapping against the wet grass. Amanda didn't care. She wanted to see how her plants were doing.

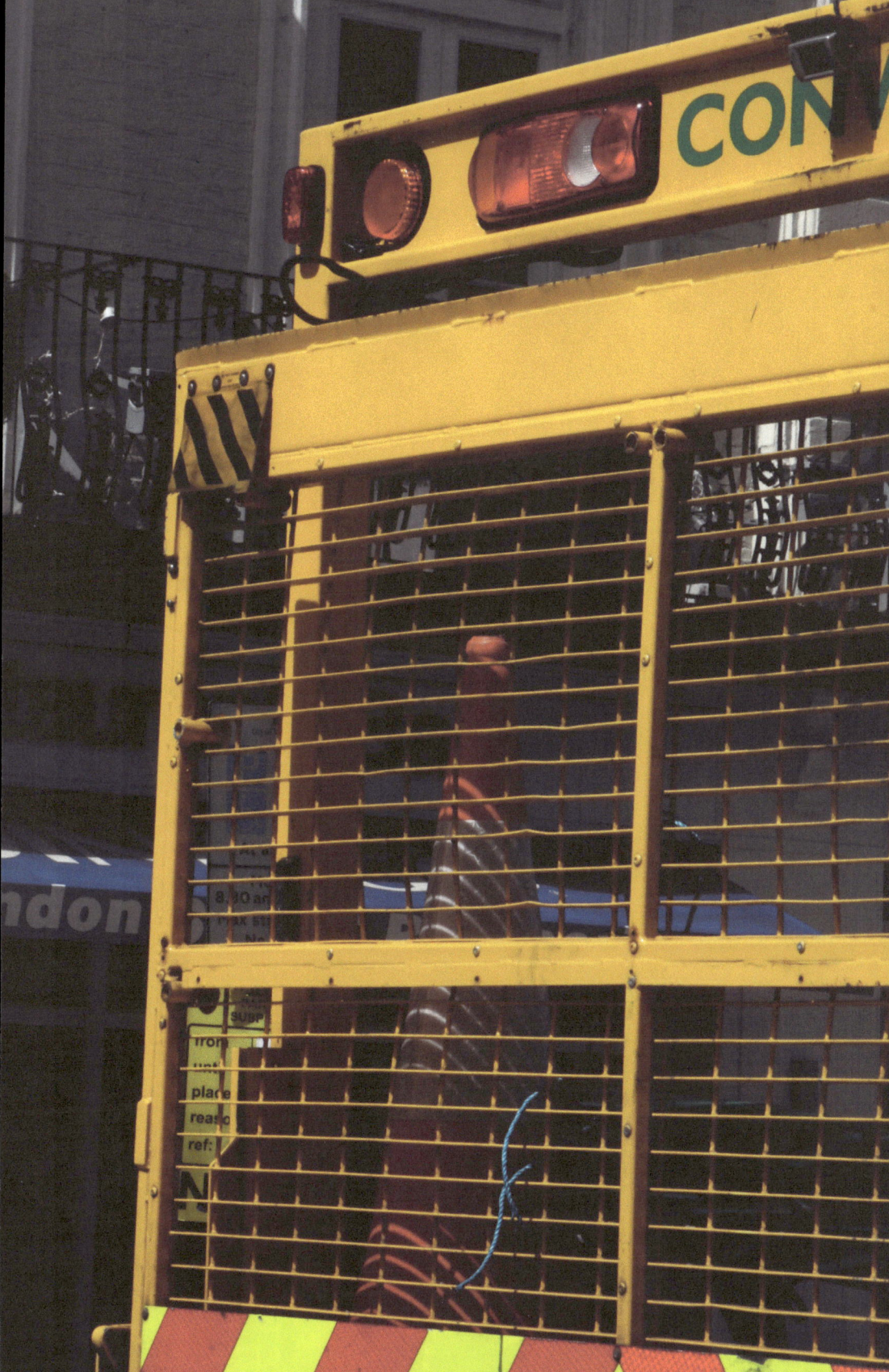

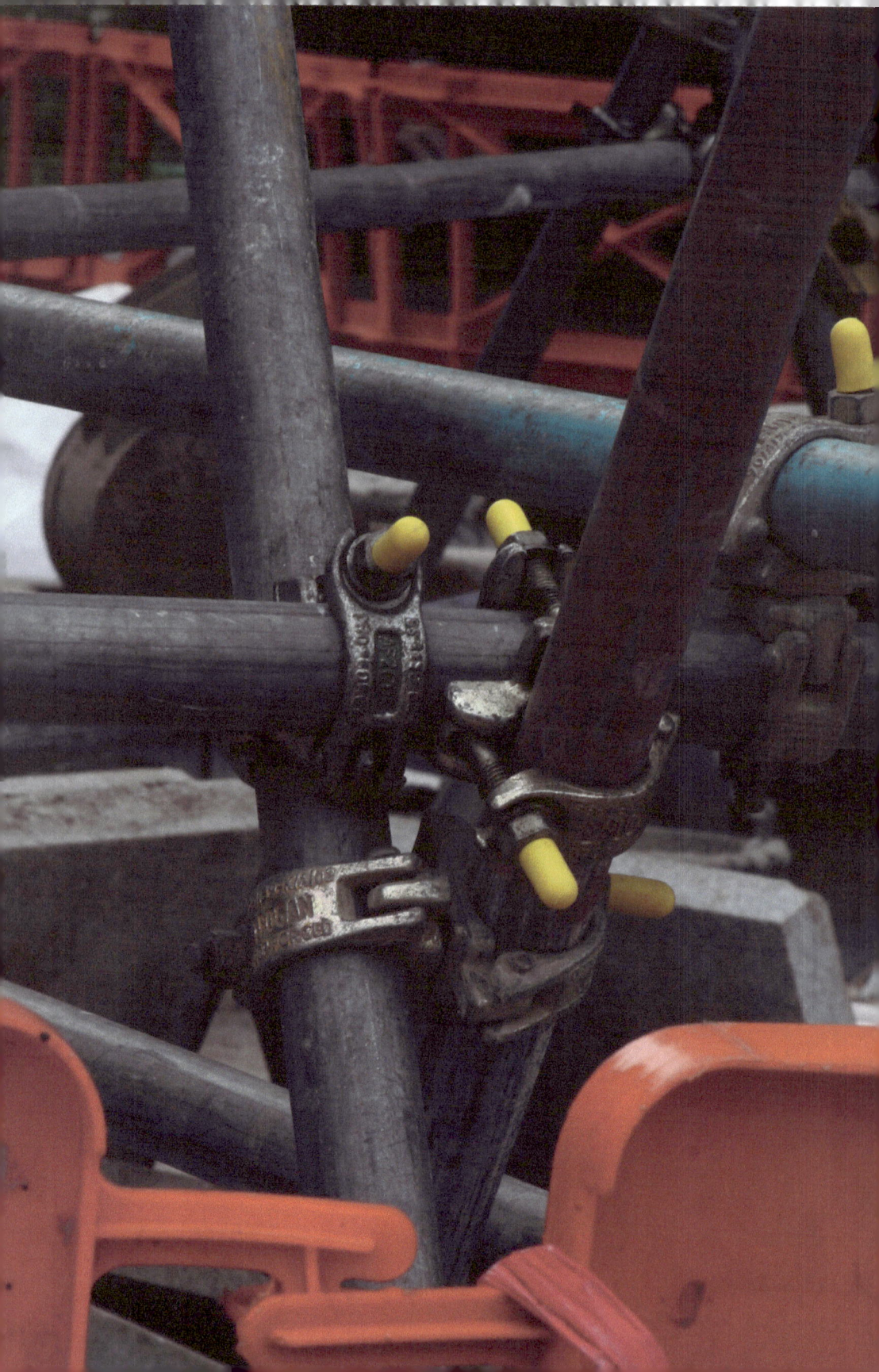

On the day before, Amanda had been stunned to see that one of the plants (which she thought was dead from not being watered) had sent out a new shoot. She was also surprised to see that the seed she had planted next to it had sprouted, overnight. Both plants had several large leaves, something that had taken her pumpkin vines a week or two.

Now when she got within view of the garden, Amanda was surprised again. The newest plant had four flowers – one fully opened, plus three buds. The shoot of the plant that had looked dead had two flowers already – smaller than the flowers on the other plant, but just as beautiful.

Amanda wished she had brought her camera. The flowers were so bright that Amanda saw them from a long ways away – a bluish aquamarine with bold red stripes and bright yellow dots.

Amanda was overwhelmed. To think that two of her plants had almost died before they flowered. How sad that would have been! These plants were more beautiful than anything Amanda had ever seen.

When Amanda reached the garden, she got another surprise. These were the most fragrant flowers she had ever seen.

As Amanda breathed in the beautiful scent, dozens of wonderful memories flooded her imagination. She could feel herself being pushed on a swing in the summer by her dad and swimming near a waterfall with friends and rolling down a steep grassy hillside with her brother. Amanda stood in the garden, smiling proudly, and taking deep breaths of the wonderful fragrance. At least she started to. She got two deep breaths when a head appeared over the tall fence next to her garden.

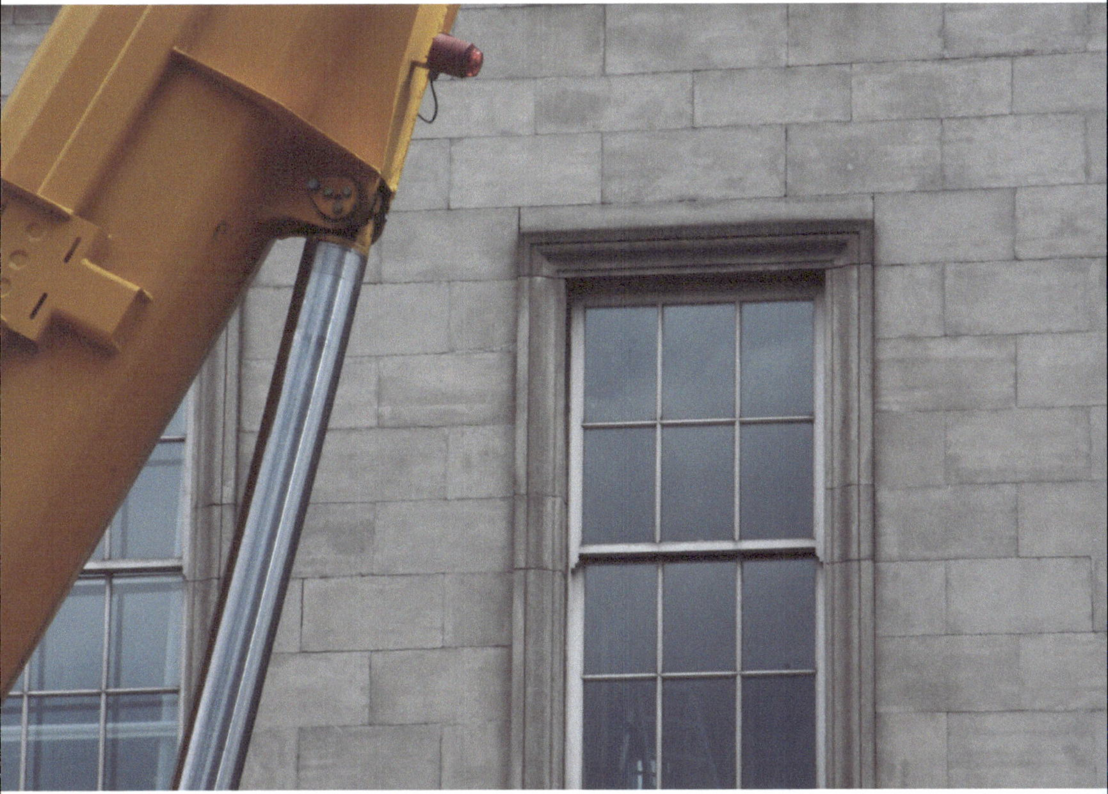

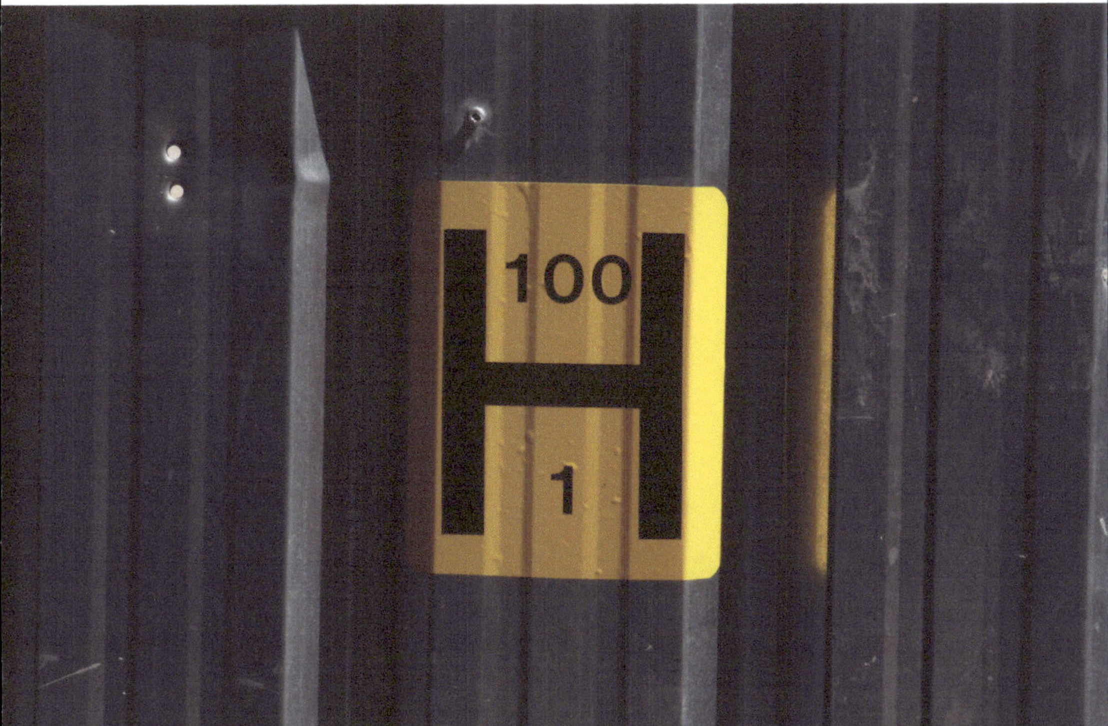

100
H
1

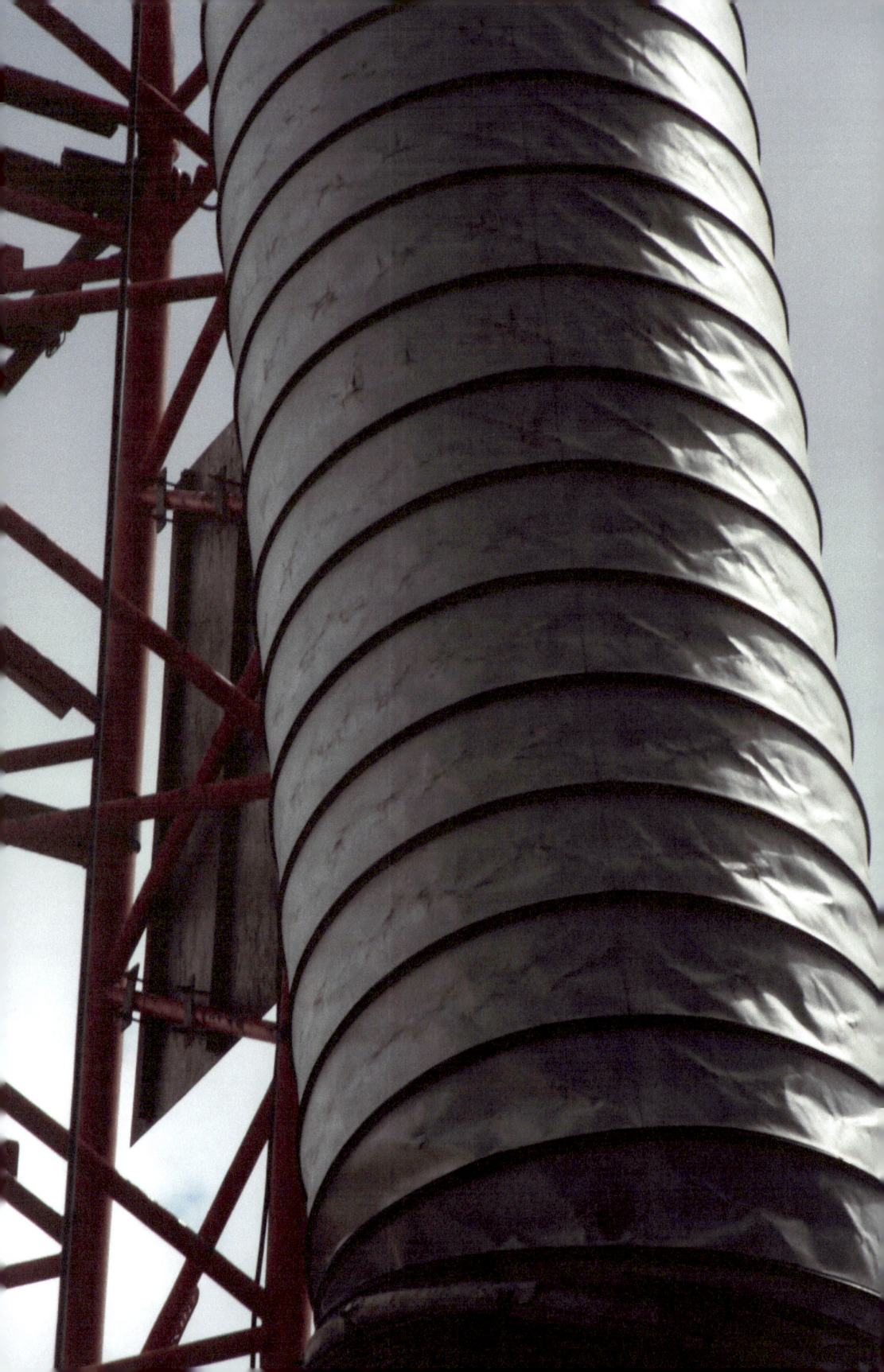

It was her neighbor. In the past he hadn't always been nice, but she had never seen him this mad before. His face was as red as a radish, and he was scowling and holding his big nose.

"Are you the one responsible for this atrocious garden?" he shouted.

The neighbor didn't sound quite as frightening as he looked since he was holding his big nose and it made his voice sound funny. Amanda might have laughed if his eyes hadn't been squinted shut in such a mean way.

"Are you responsible?" he yelled. "Is this your garden?"

"Yes," said Amanda. "It is."

"Your flowers are stinking up my yard," he shouted. "They're stinking up my whole *house*. I can't even breathe! You *must* get rid of those flowers at once!"

Amanda was shocked. "I can't do *that!"* she said. "They were a present from my grandfather."

The neighbor harrumphed. "I can see why he wanted to get rid of them. But you *must* get them out of your garden. At once. Do it now or I will call the police."

He had been yelling so loudly and had such an angry look that Amanda started to cry. Her beautiful plants! How could he not like them? And the beautiful smell! How could he not like *it?*

"And stop crying," he shouted. "You have no right to poison the air of your neighbors. I'm going to form a committee to get your whole family expelled from the neighborhood!"

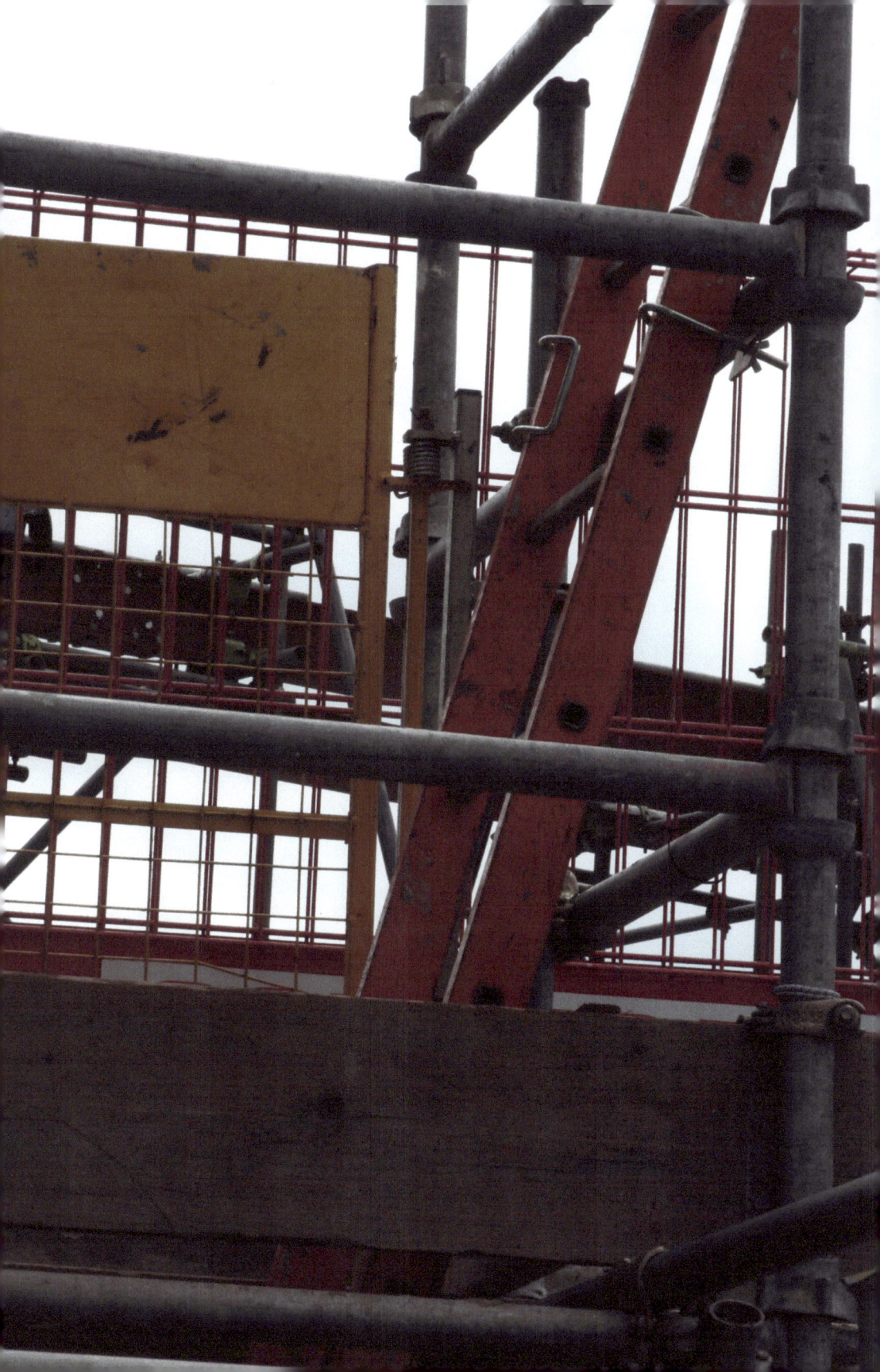

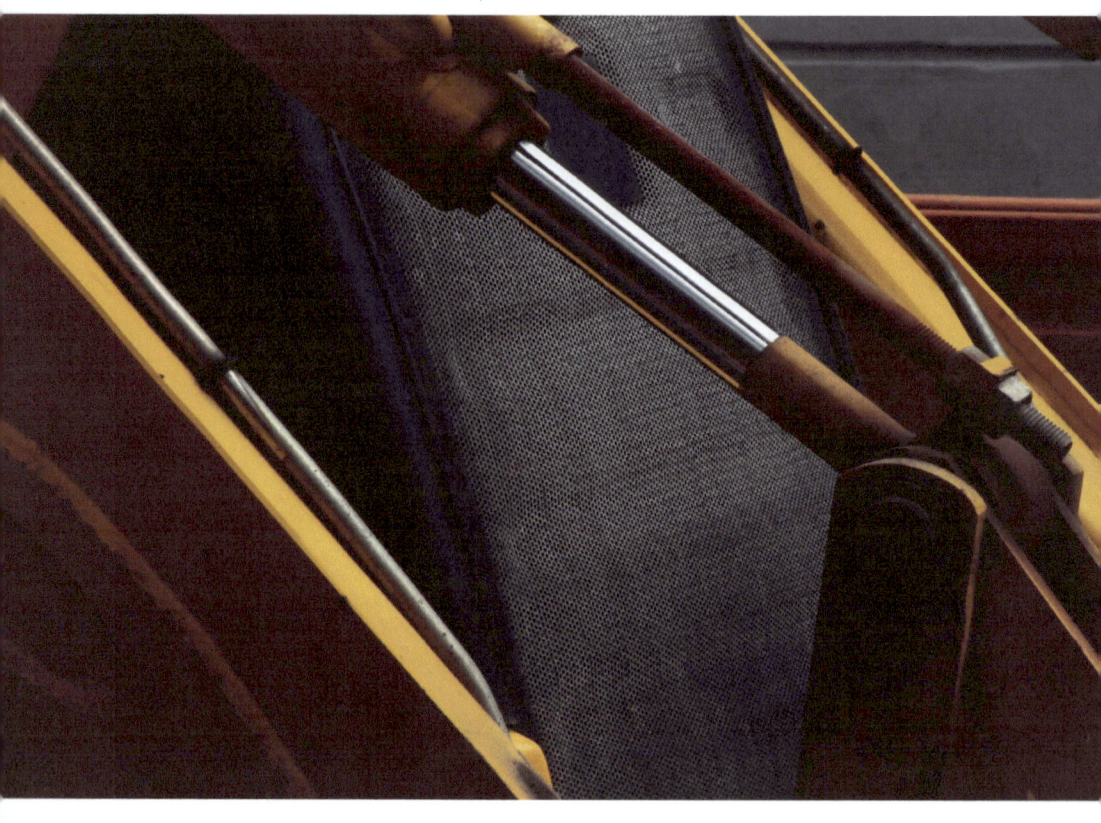

A year ago, Amanda had been a little afraid of her grandfather. Then she had gotten to know him, and now she was not afraid of him at all. But Amanda didn't think getting to know her neighbor would make him less scary.

Amanda backed up slowly toward her house. Her neighbor's face disappeared below the fence. But she heard him yell once more as he disappeared. "Get rid of those plants or there will be trouble!"

Inside the house, Amanda told her mom. Her mom thought Amanda must be exaggerating. She didn't think the neighbor could have been so mean, especially after she went out to the garden and saw how beautiful the flowers were and how wonderfully they smelled.

"Are you sure, Amanda?" she asked. "Are you sure you're not exaggerating, just a little?"

That afternoon their doorbell rang. Two neighbors were at the door.

"We can't stay," one said when Amanda's mom opened the door. "We just want you to know we don't support what everybody else is saying."

"Or what they plan to do," said the other.

"No. Especially not *that.*"

"What are they saying? What do they plan to do?" Amanda's mom asked. But the neighbors wouldn't answer.

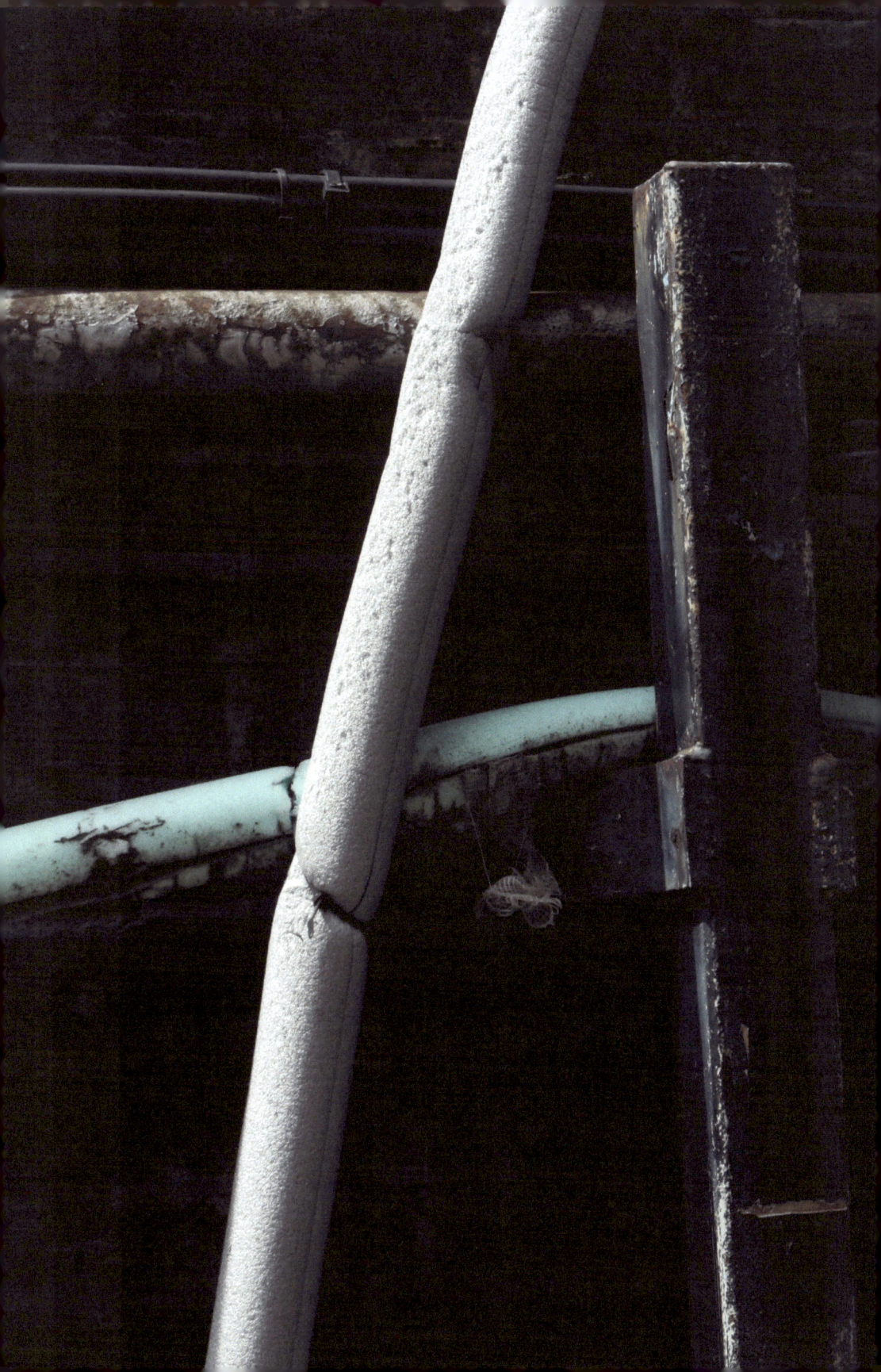

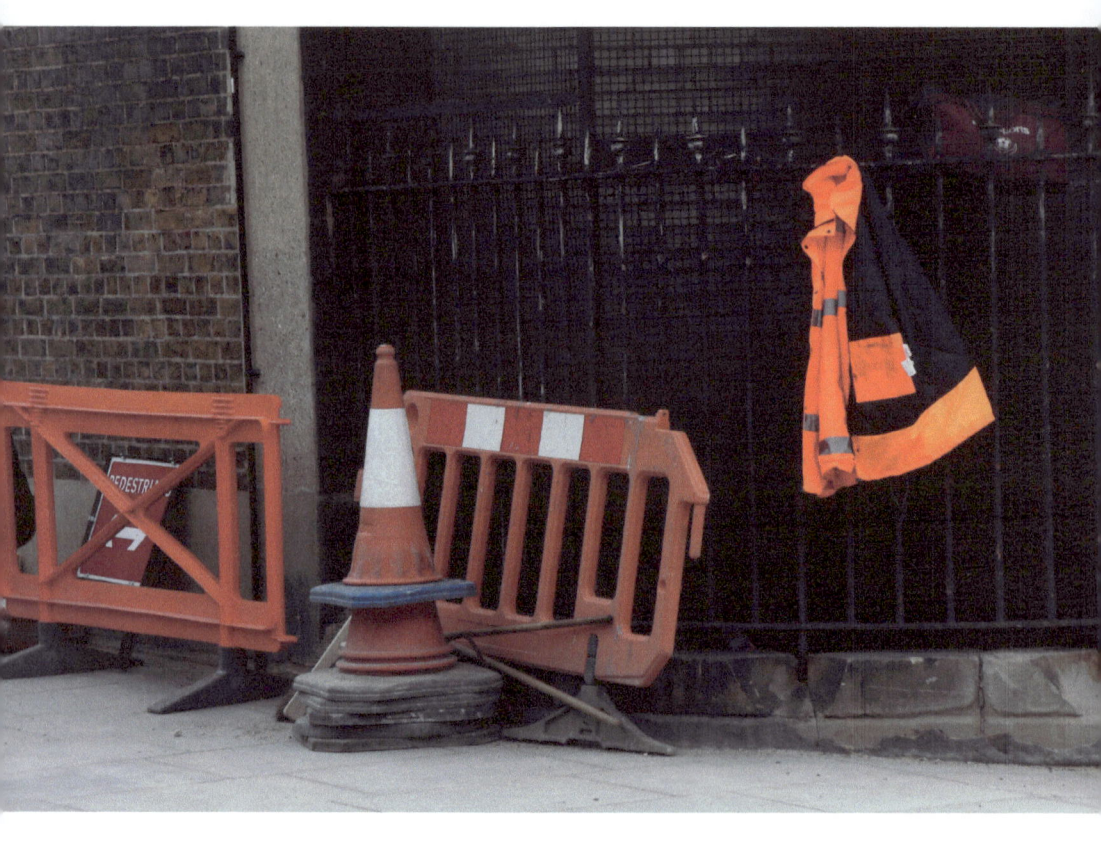

"We have to go," one said.

"Before we're seen," said the other. "But we *do* like the pleasant smell that's filling all the neighborhood."

"Delightful!" said the first with a smile. Then the smile left her face. "Too bad the others are so *mad*."

They turned to leave. Amanda's mom thanked them and slowly closed the door.

"What now?" she wondered. She didn't know.

That afternoon Amanda went out to her garden to think. All the flowers had opened up, and the smell was even more beautiful than she remembered.

On impulse, Amanda reached into the air and touched something soft, cold and squishy. It felt like the glop inside a pumpkin that surrounds the seeds. Amanda grabbed hold and pulled. Nothing happened.

She reached into the air with *both* hands and pulled again. Nothing. She pulled harder. It seemed to move slightly. She gave it one last tug, harder than before.

Out of thin air she pulled a huge glop of seeds and cold, stringy mush. It was green, and the seeds were an inch long, so whatever this was, it wasn't pumpkin seeds. Her grandfather had said this was the miracle she had wanted.

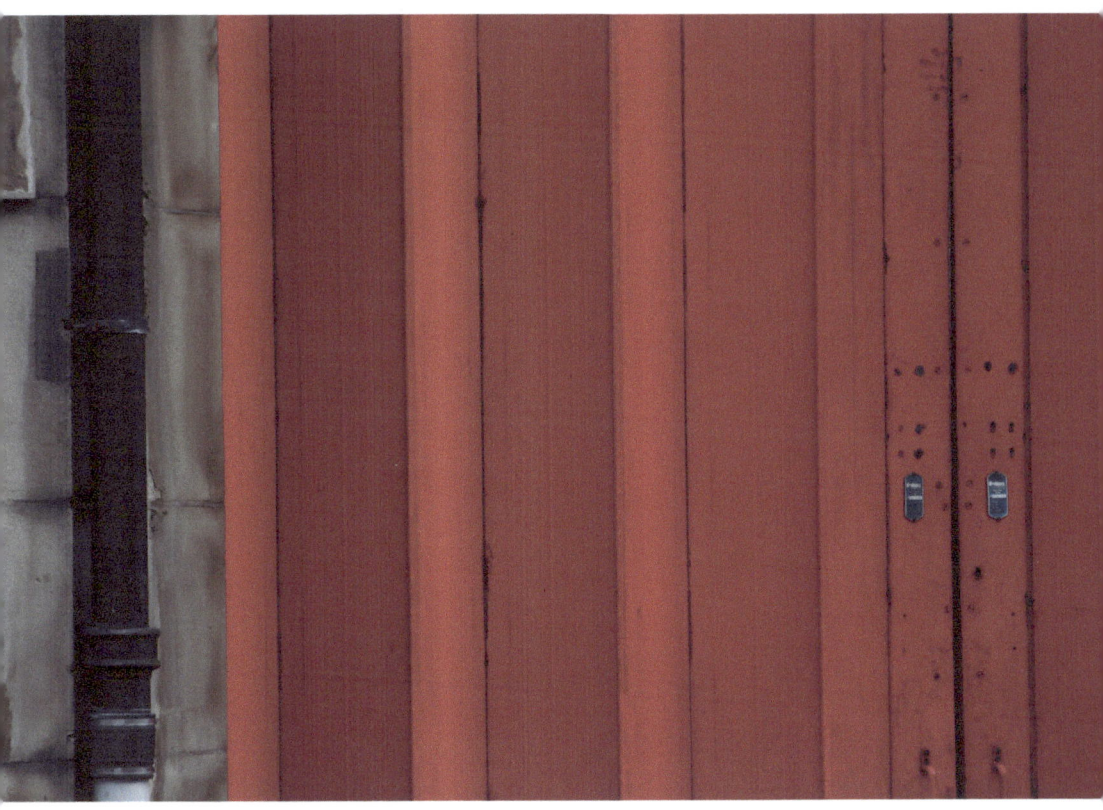

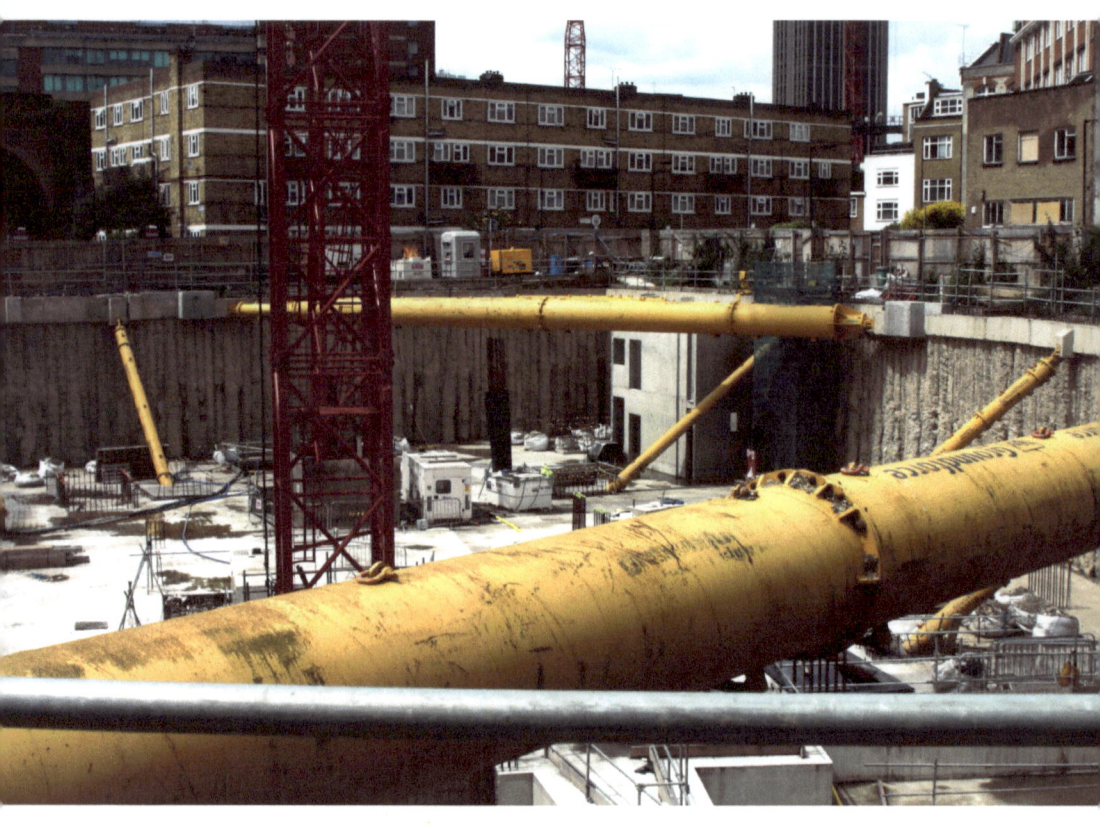

Amanda prepared the soil, then carefully planted the new seeds in her garden. She stood looking at the spot for quite a while, smiling, thinking about her miracle, wondering how fast it would grow. Then she walked away whistling, even though her hands were still covered in the green glop that she had been avoiding for days.

She had planted her miracle! Things were looking up!

The next morning when Amanda awoke, she threw the covers into a heap at the foot of the bed. Then she changed her mind and pulled them back up over the bed so it would look nicer. She dressed quickly and slipped on her shoes without lacing them and ran out to the garden and – long before she got there – stopped.

Her plants were gone. She was twenty feet away and she could see where her plants *should* have been, but they were gone.

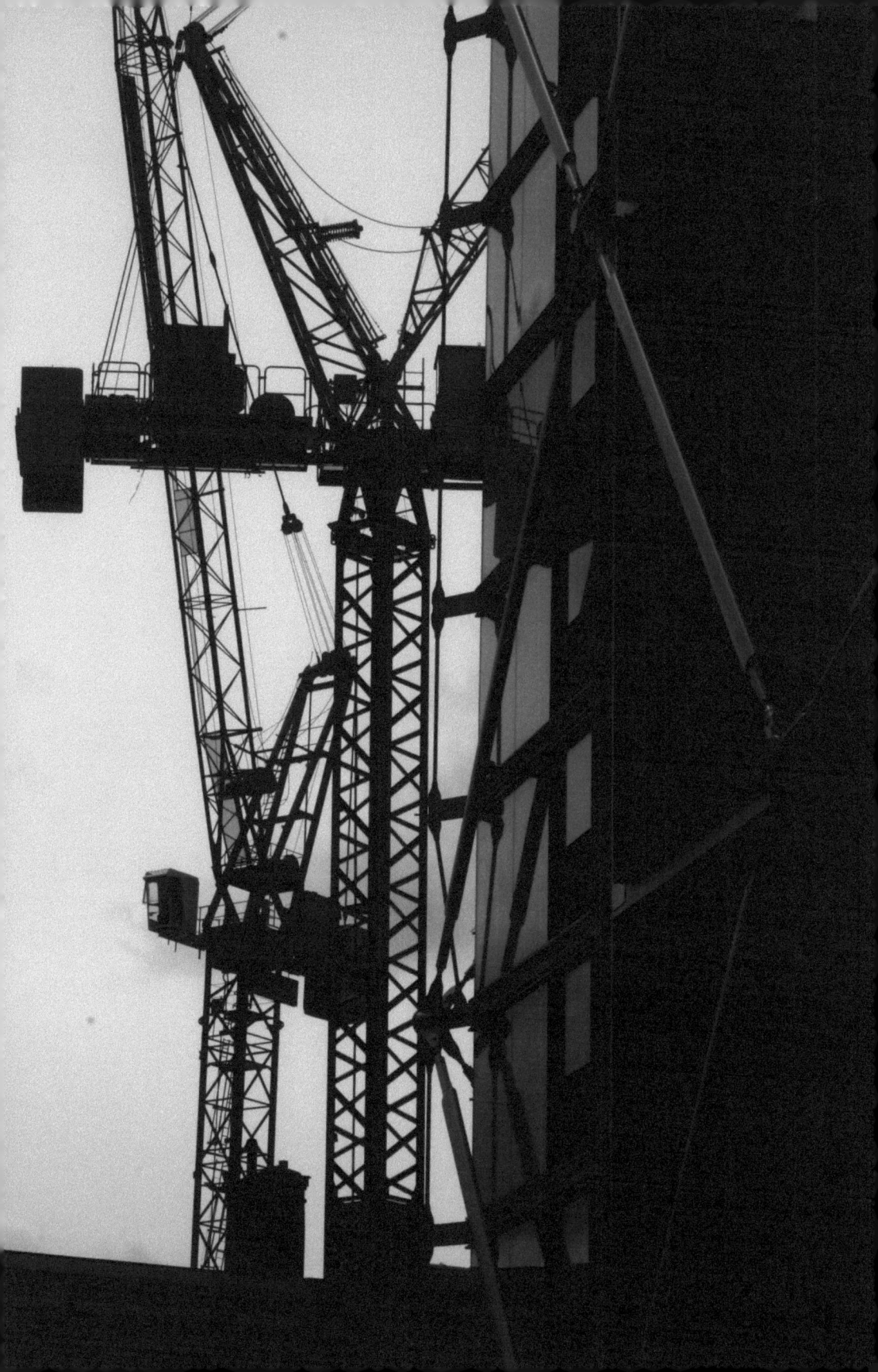

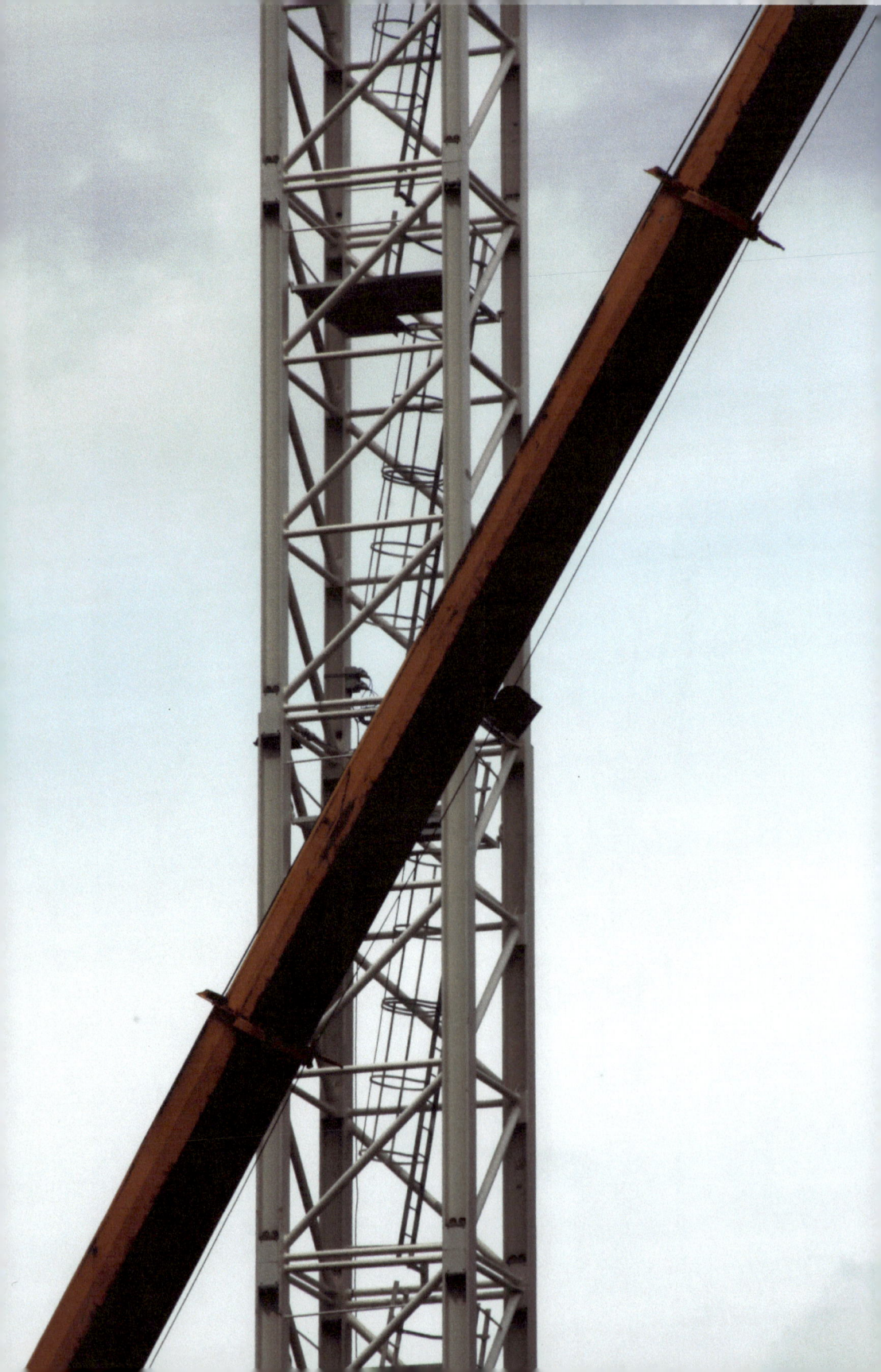

"Mom?" she called.

Inside the house, Amanda's mom looked up, then raced to put on her own shoes and run to her daughter. She knew that tone of voice. That was how Amanda sounded just before she was going to cry.

Amanda walked slowly toward the garden. Her garden. Or what *used* to be her garden.

Amanda's mom ran and got to the garden just as Amanda did, saw everything at a glance, and reached out to hold her daughter.

"Oh, Amanda," she said, wiping a tear from her eye.

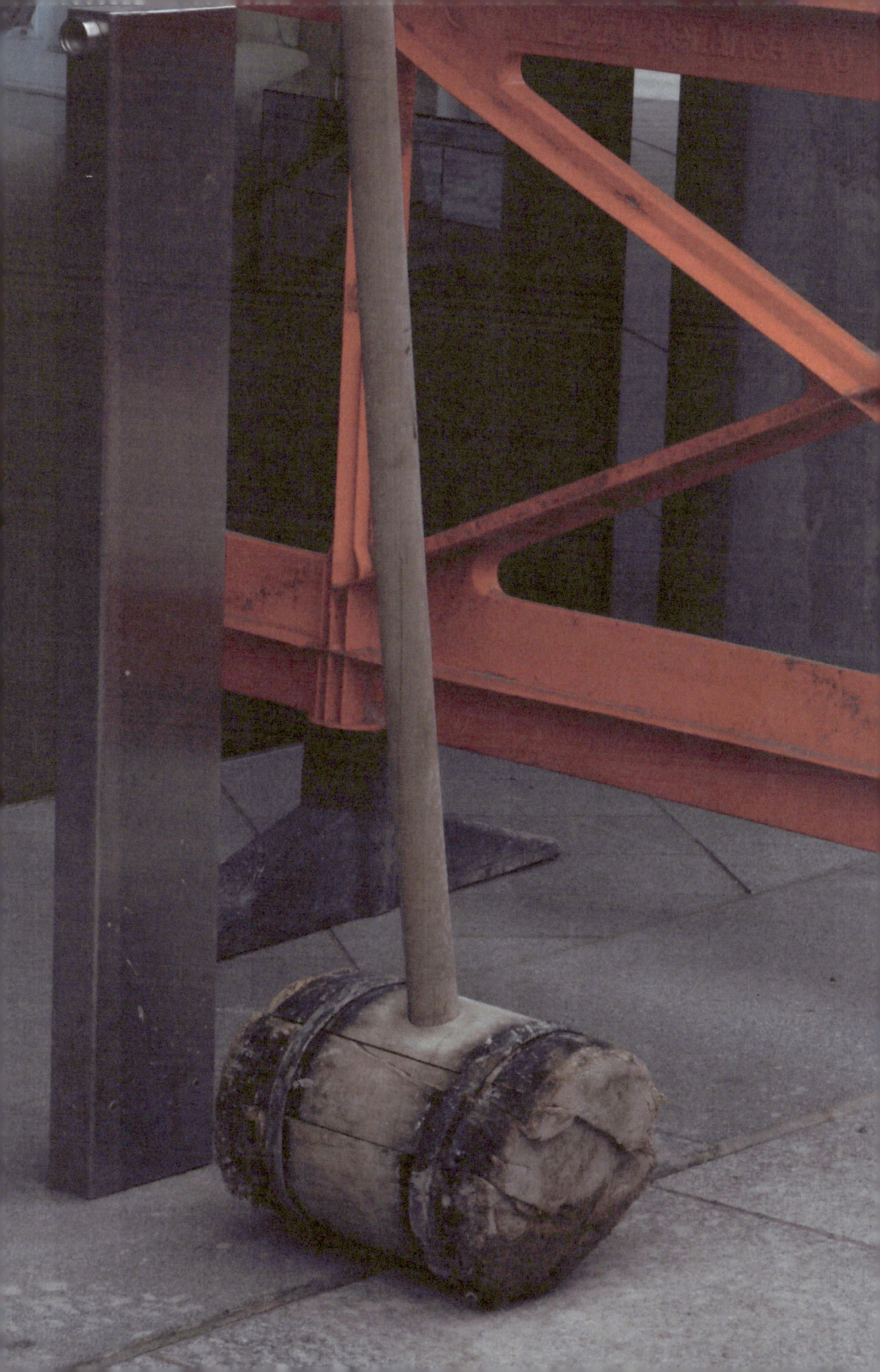

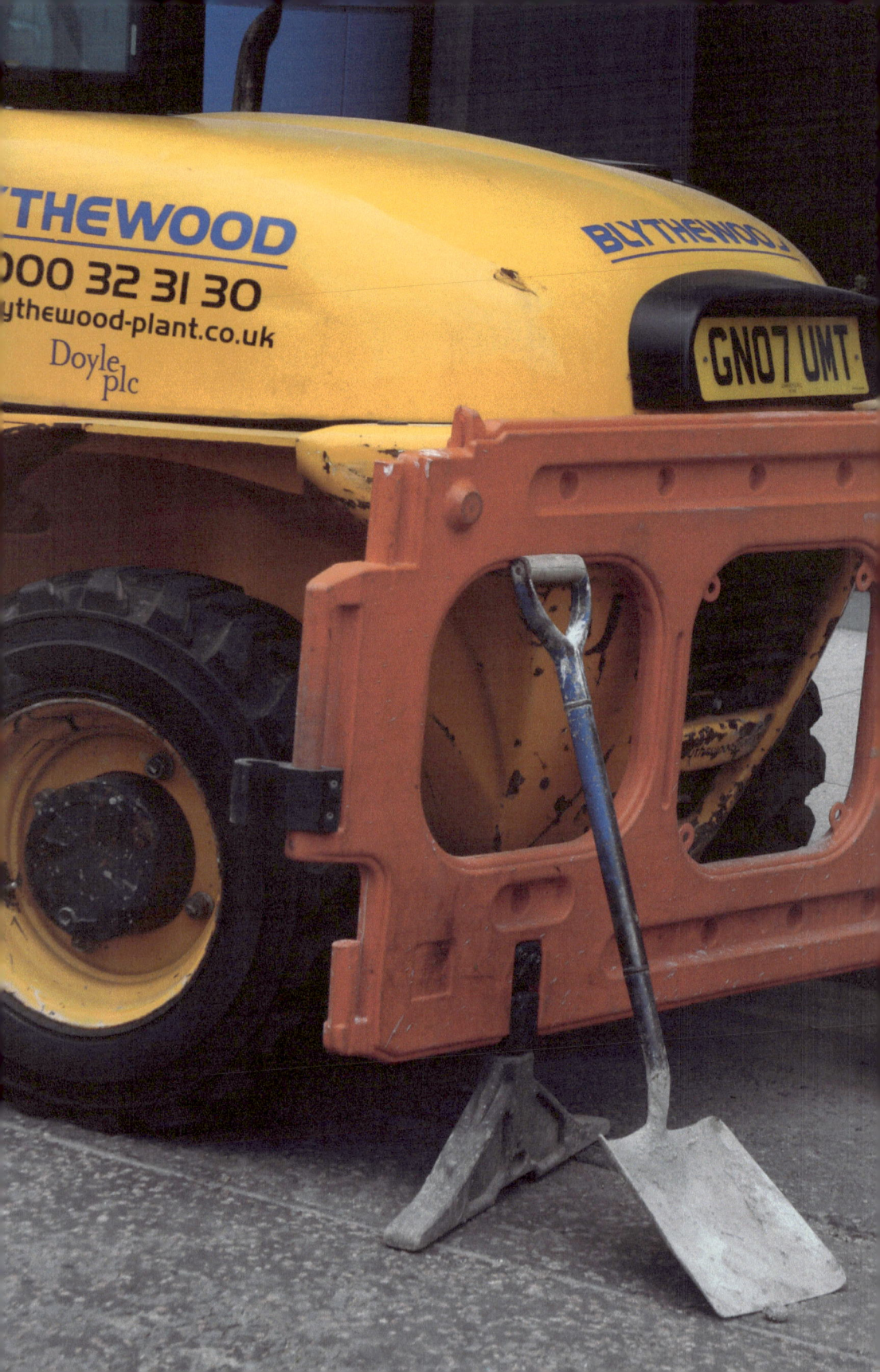

The pumpkin vines and watermelon vines had barely started to sprout, but they had all been stomped into the ground. It looked like they had been trampled by several careless people.

The porcelain figures Amanda had put in the garden near her plants had all been smashed to bits. Tiny fragments of broken porcelain covered the ground. Amanda could see only one porcelain figure that survived, a small black spider that was partially hidden by a rock.

But that wasn't the worst.

The mysterious plants from her grandfather had been hacked into bits. Their beautiful flowers had been shredded, their petals stomped into the dirt.

The sprouts from the green seeds that Amanda had planted the day before had been treated the worst. They were smashed into a green pulpy mass.

Amanda burst into tears. "My garden!" she wailed. "My pumpkins! My watermelons! My figurines! My plants from grandpa! Even my new plant! Everything is smashed into bits!"

Amanda's mom held her and they both stood looking at the scene for a long time. There was no reason to rush away. They stayed long enough to take it all in.

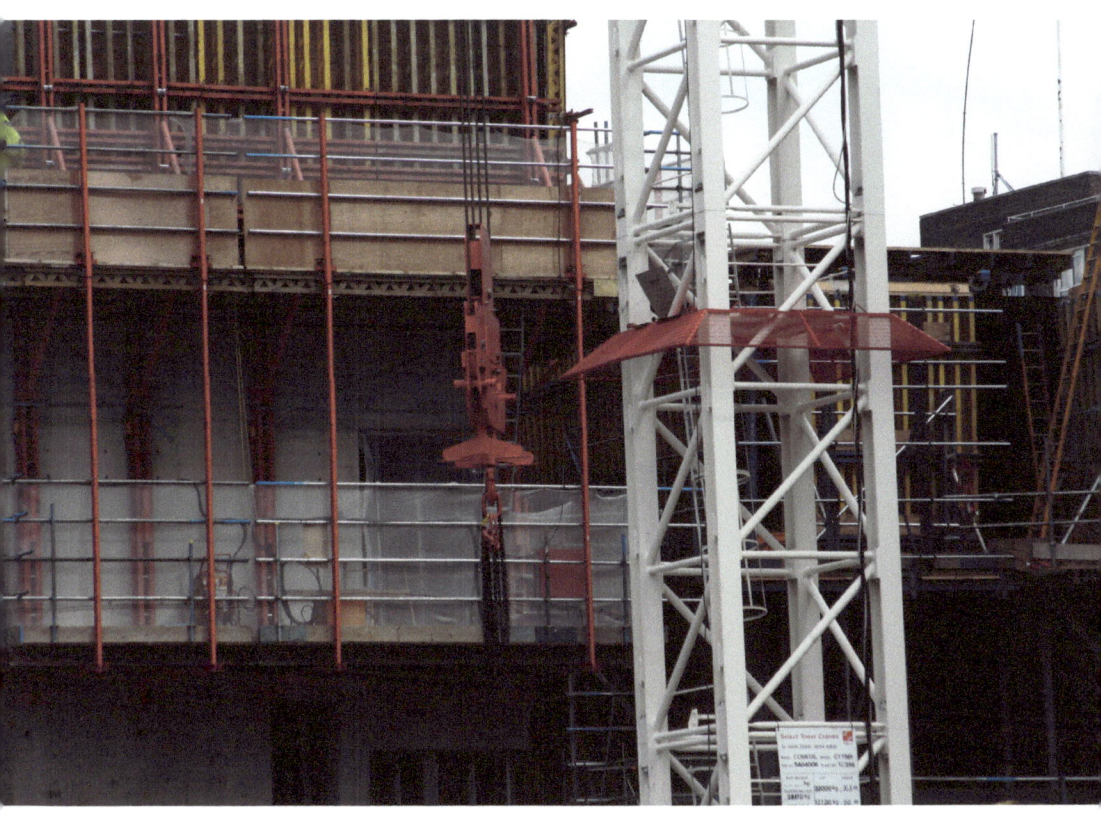

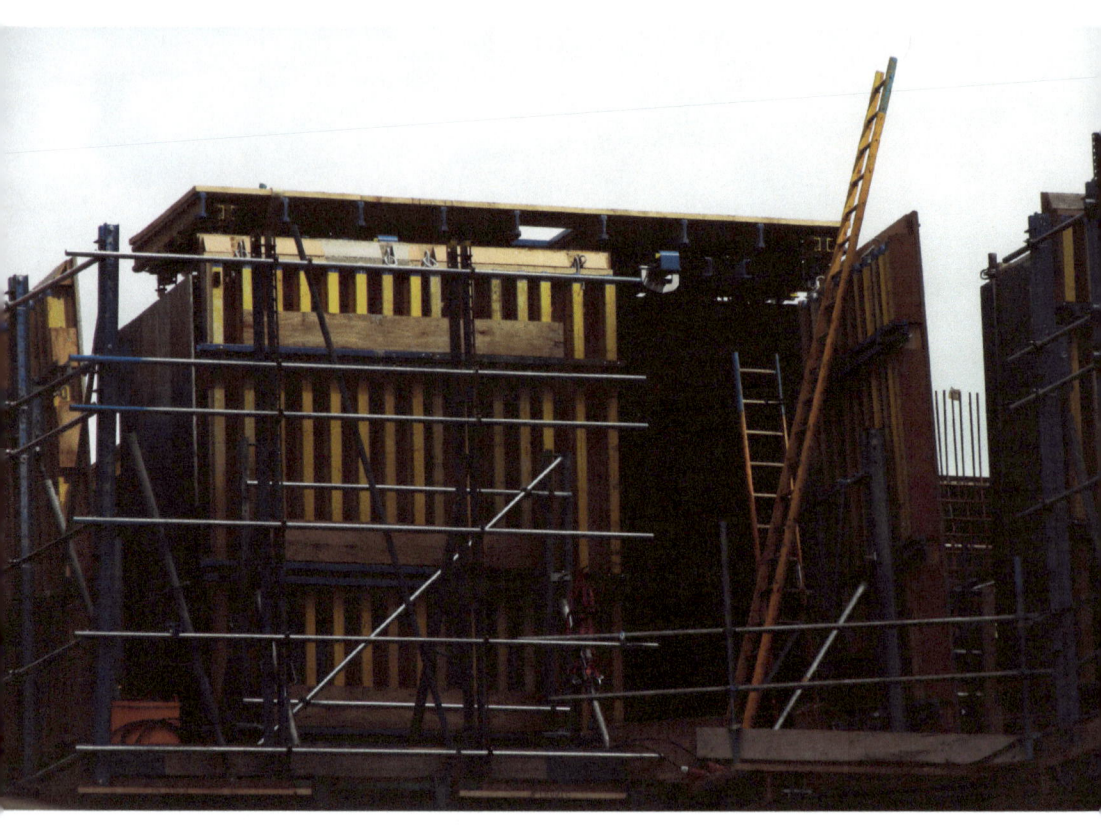

After she had cried a while, Amanda knew what to do next.

"I have to call grandpa," she said.

Amanda's mom nodded, and they walked back to the kitchen arm in arm.

Amanda had just started telling her grandfather what had happened when he laughed. The first laugh just slipped out. Then he let go and laughed and laughed and laughed.

It was so unexpected Amanda thought he probably hadn't heard what she'd said. She stared over.

"Oh, Amanda," he said, laughing again. "I know you're sad. I don't mean to laugh. But your poor neighbor. He's *not* going to like what he did." Then he laughed again. Finally he quit laughing long enough to explain.

"Listen, Amanda," he said. "I'm very sorry all your beautiful porcelain figures are smashed. But you're getting better and better at creating them, and you'll be able to quickly replace them with even nicer ones. So they don't matter so much, even though it's too bad they were smashed.

"And all those chopped up plants from the seeds I gave you? They're all going to sprout. That's how you get more of those plants if you don't have seeds. Your neighbor didn't like your garden before, but he's *really* not going to like it tomorrow!"

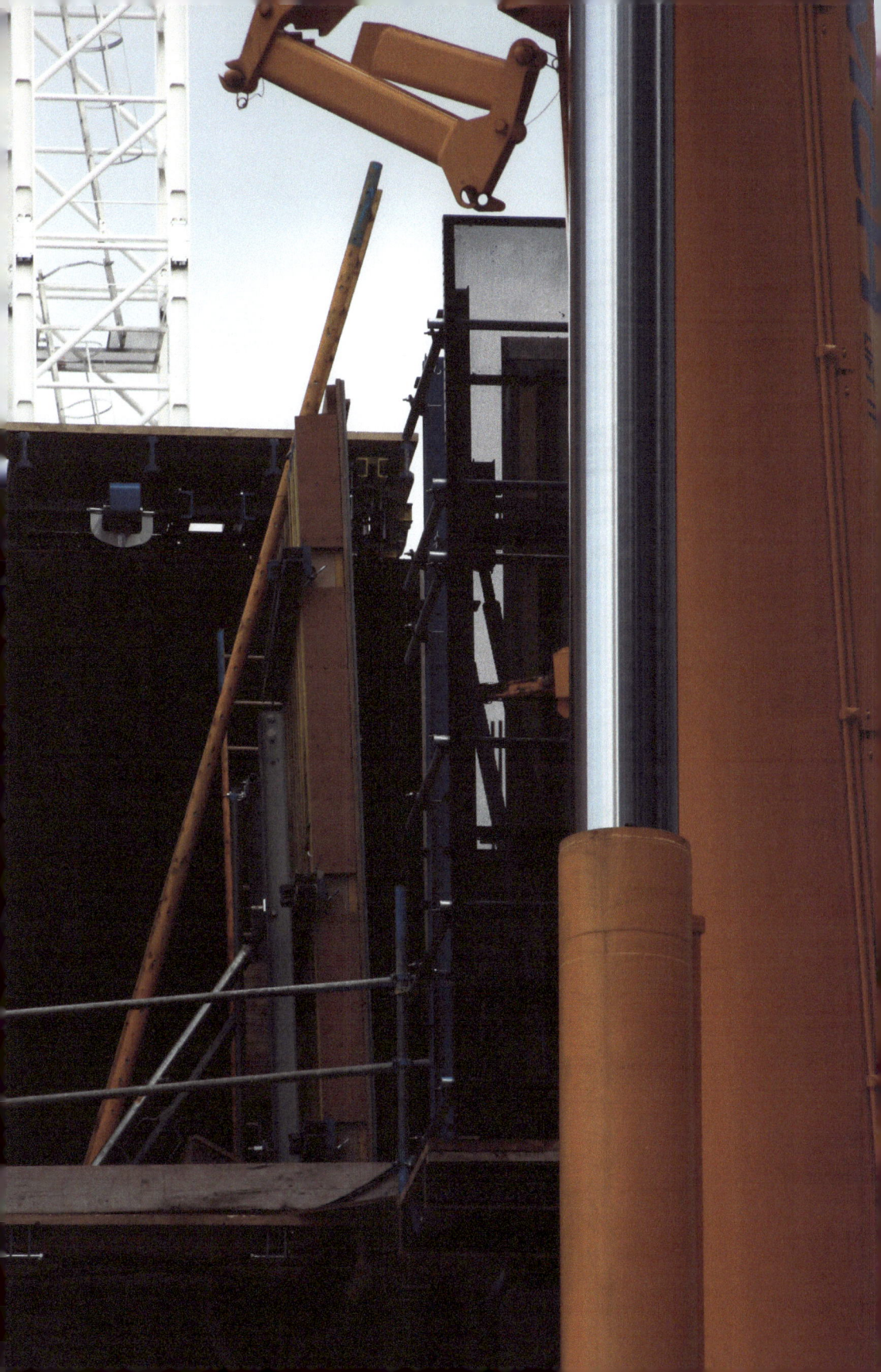

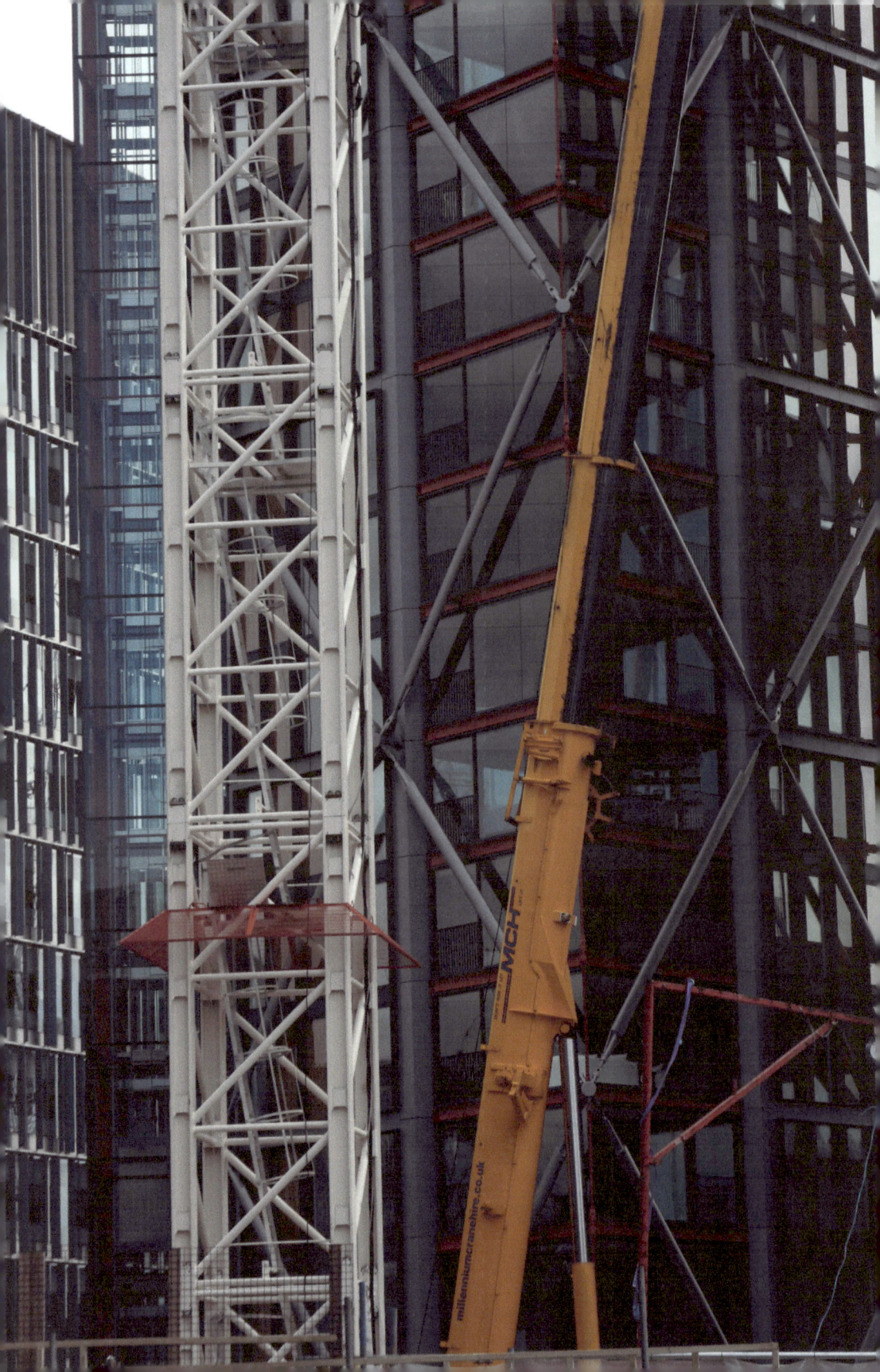

Then Amanda's grandfather got serious. "I know you're shocked and sad to see your garden smashed like this. I'm sorry I laughed when you feel so bad. But your neighbor has *no* idea what he's done. You'll see tomorrow.

"You don't have to be sad about anything, Amanda. Your garden, your plants, your porcelain, your miracle – they may look smashed up, but don't worry about it. It's all going to work out. I can promise you that.

"My own garden got hacked up once or twice when I lived in the city, so I've seen what happens next. You don't have to worry at all."

He paused for a moment.

"Amanda, I moved this far out of town to get away from neighbors like yours. It would probably be better if you and your mom came to stay with me for a few days. Bring a few of those cuttings – the smashed up plants – we'll put them in my garden next to the plant of yours that's doing so well. But be sure to leave a few cuttings in your garden for your neighbor. They'll sprout tonight and be twice as big and four times as fragrant tomorrow." He laughed again.

"I wish I could see your neighbor's face tomorrow. His house is going to be *filled* with perfume. Plus, he'll never get that beautiful scent off the tools he used to chop up your plants."

Then he paused again.

"When you and your mom come out, you may as well invite your grandmother," he said. "It's about time we got the whole family together again – at least for a day or two."

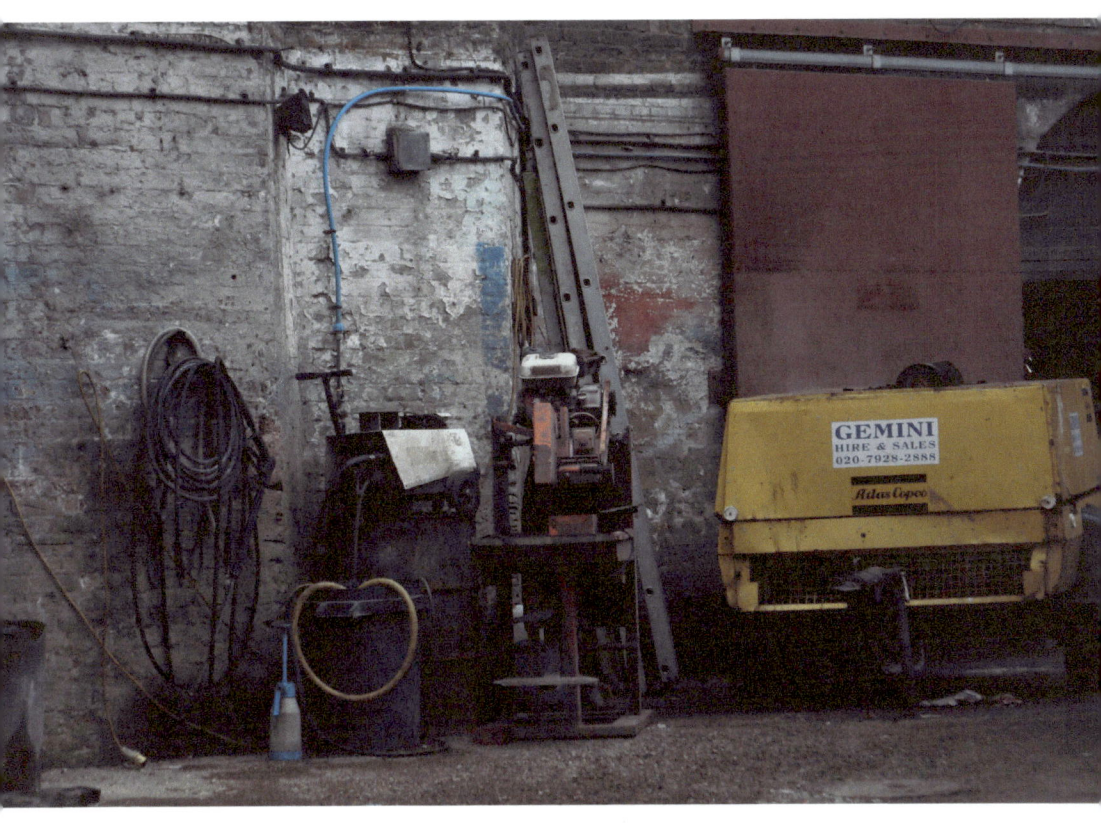

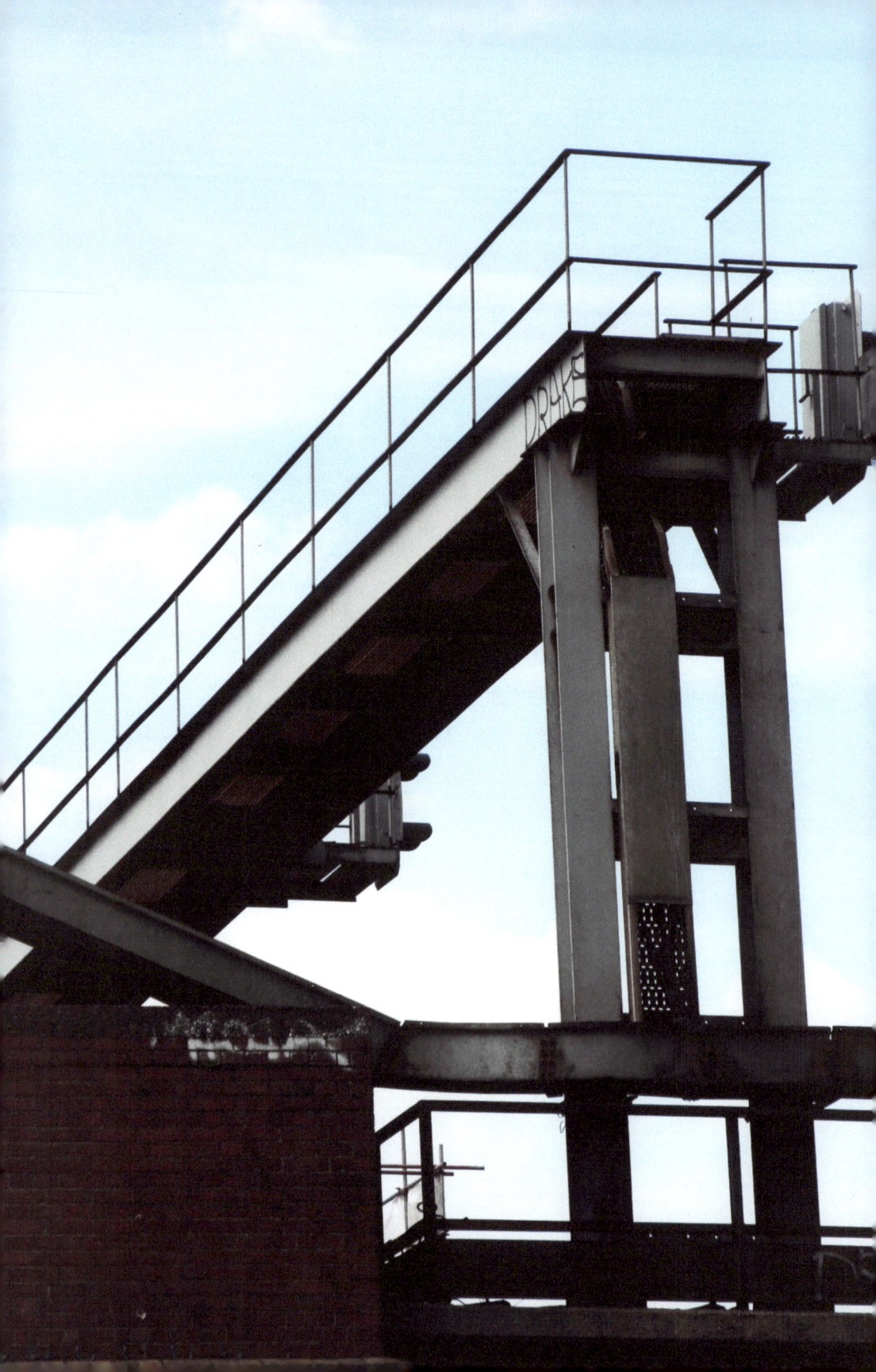

Amanda smiled. This day was turning out far better than she expected. Maybe she'd get her miracle after all.

Reflection questions

Sometimes you will face angry neighbors, even if what you are doing is something wonderful, like growing a beautiful, fragrant plant.

What should you do if a neighbor is angry?

What should you do if what you are working on gets destroyed?

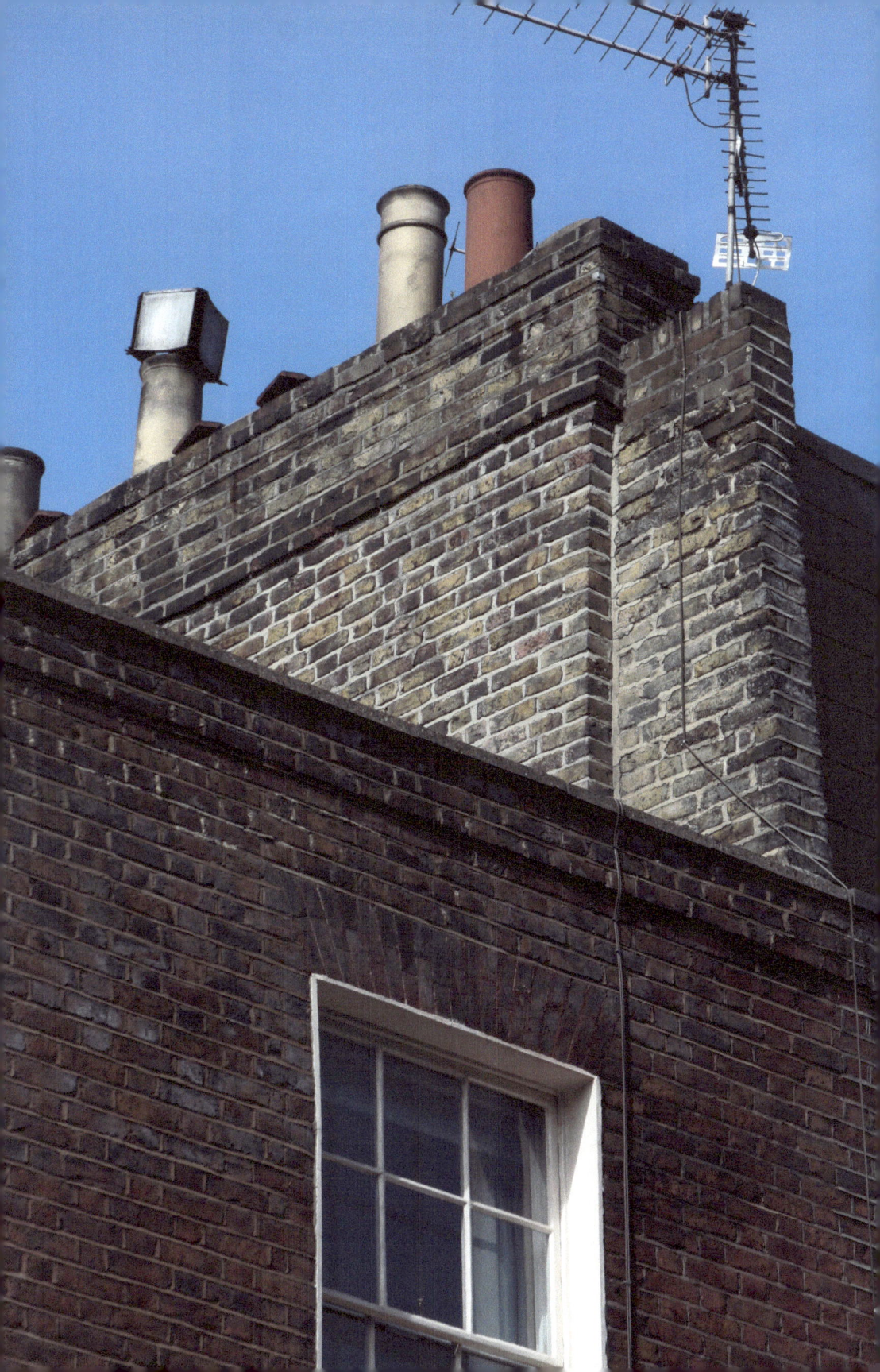

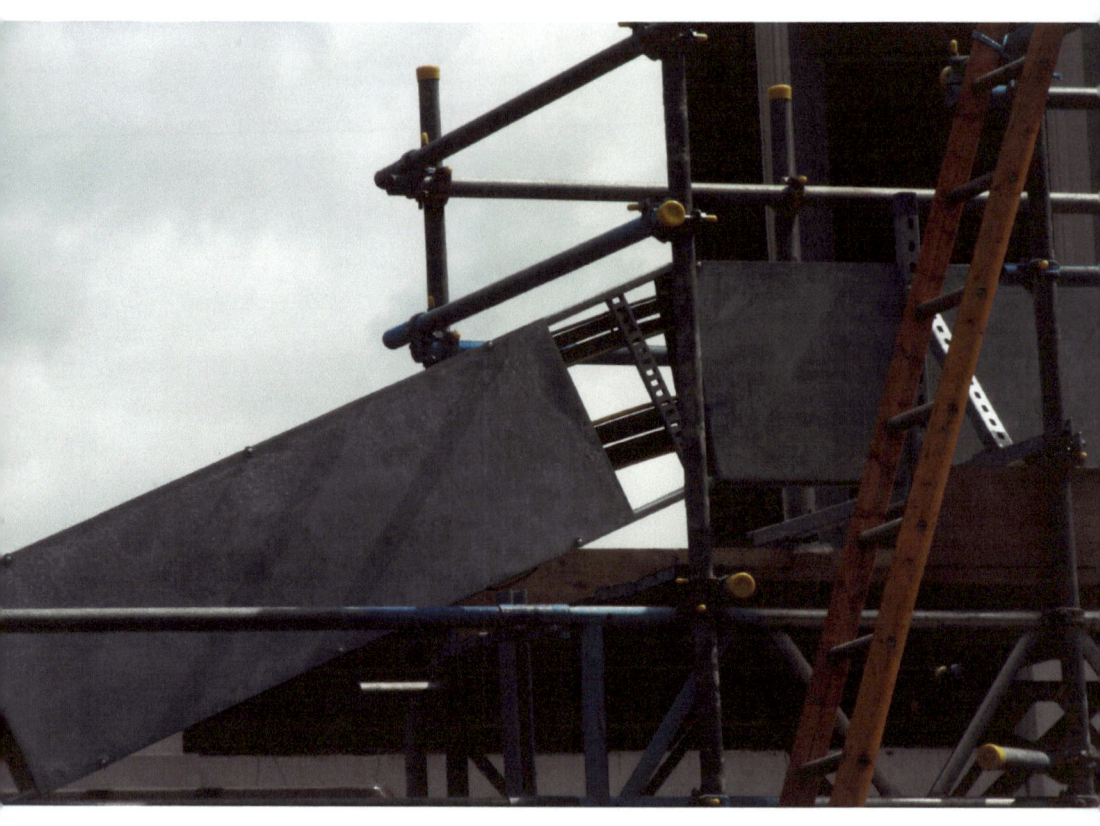

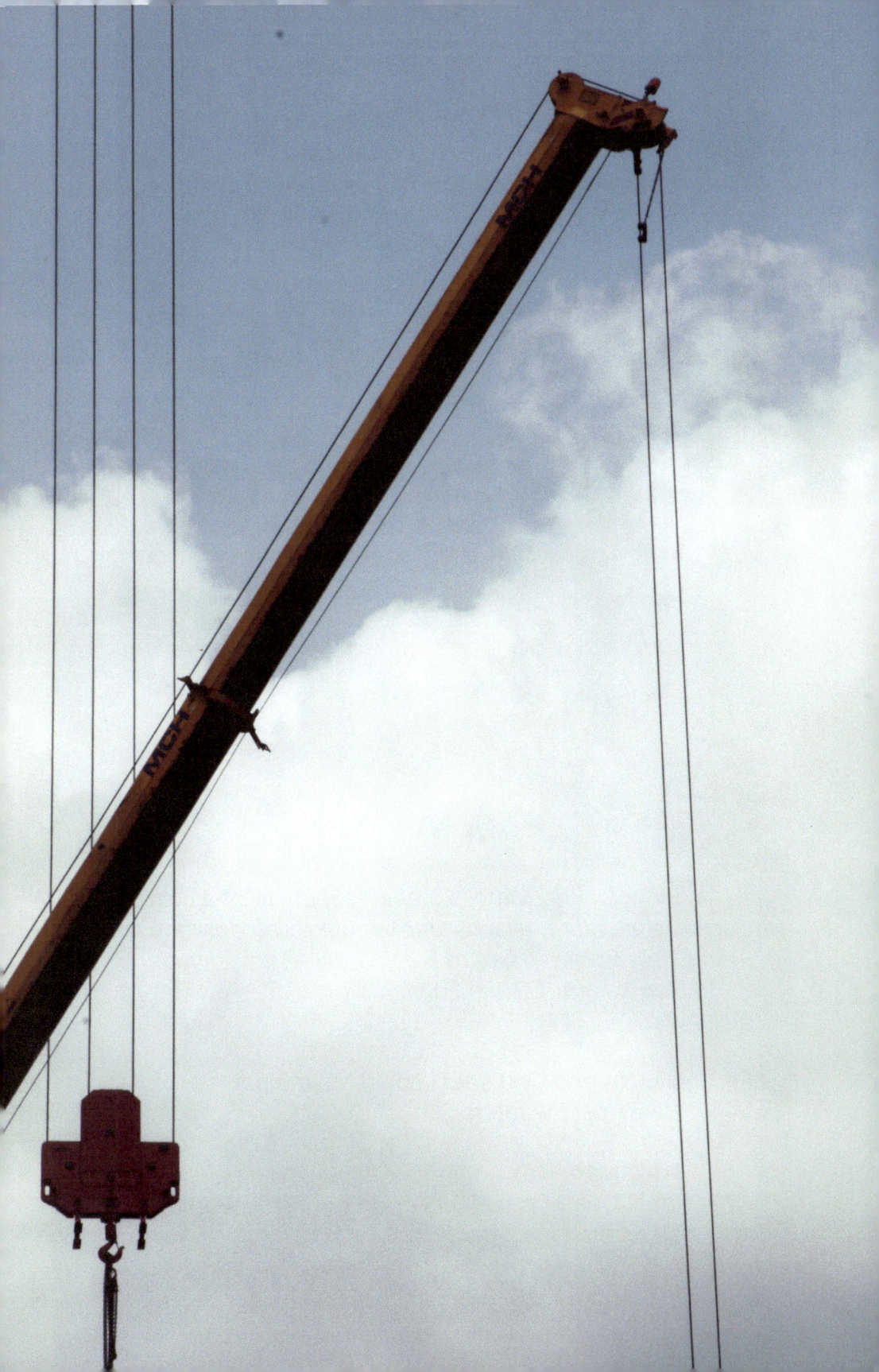

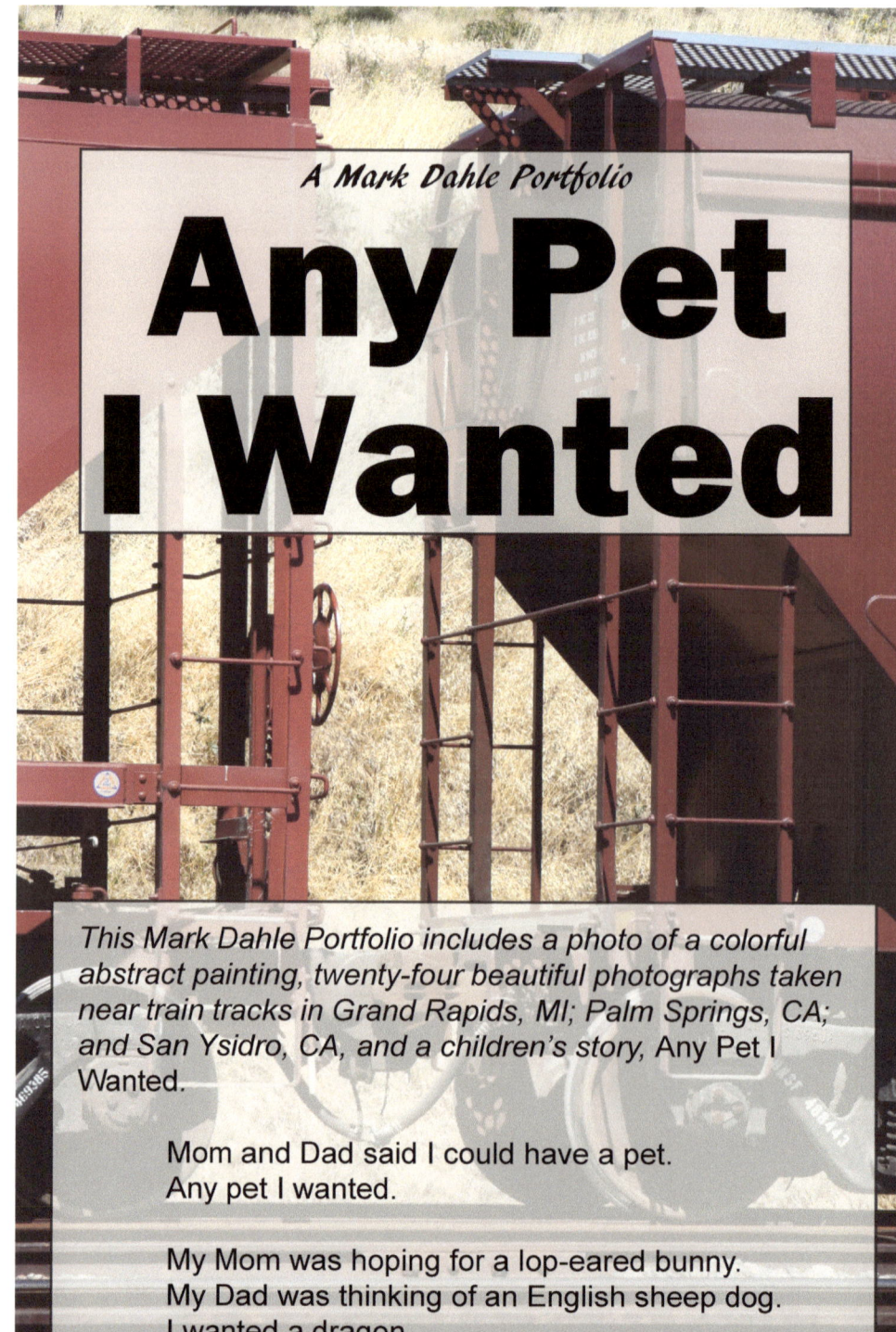

A Mark Dahle Portfolio

Any Pet
I Wanted

This Mark Dahle Portfolio includes a photo of a colorful abstract painting, twenty-four beautiful photographs taken near train tracks in Grand Rapids, MI; Palm Springs, CA; and San Ysidro, CA, and a children's story, Any Pet I Wanted.

Mom and Dad said I could have a pet.
Any pet I wanted.

My Mom was hoping for a lop-eared bunny.
My Dad was thinking of an English sheep dog.
I wanted a dragon.

This Mark Dahle Portfolio includes a colorful painting, twenty-nine beautiful photographs from Ketchikan, Alaska, and a story about a girl who wanted a miracle.

Amanda's room was on the second floor, and she had a clear view of the fence ablaze, with the flames getting closer and closer to the house.

"Fire!" she yelled. "The fence is on fire! Mom! The fence is on fire!"

A Mark Dahle Portfolio

Amanda Gets A Miracle

(#5 in the series "Amanda Wanted A Miracle")

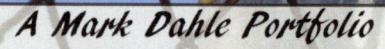

A Mark Dahle Portfolio

The Grasshopper And The Flea

Some Things Never Change

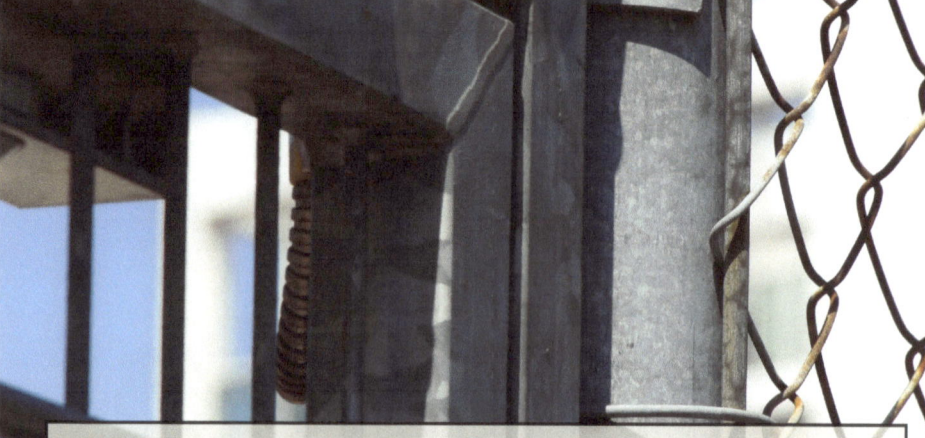

This Mark Dahle Portfolio includes a colorful painting, twenty-six beautiful photographs of fences in Basel, Switzerland, and a story about Aesop having remarkable difficulties writing a story.

Aesop liked the morals at the end of his stories to stay put. But he had just written about a grasshopper and a flea, and the moral was hopping around.

www.ingramcontent.com/pod-product-compliance
Lightning Source LLC
Chambersburg PA
CBHW040917180526
45159CB00002BA/508